TALKABOUT
Water

Text: Angela Webb
Photography: Chris Fairclough

Franklin Watts
London/New York/Sydney/Toronto

©1986 Franklin Watts

First published in Great Britain by

Franklin Watts
12a Golden Square
London W1

First published in the USA by

Franklin Watts Inc
387 Park Avenue South
New York 10016

ISBN: UK edition 0 86313 476 9

ISBN: US edition 0–531–10372–2
Library of Congress
Catalog Card No: 87–50231

Editor: Ruth Thomson
Design: Edward Kinsey
Additional Photographs: Zefa

Typesetting: Keyspools Ltd
Printed in Italy

About this book

This book has been written for young children—in the playgroup, school and at home.

Its aim is to increase children's awareness of the world around them and to promote thought and discussion about topics of scientific interest.

The book draws on examples from a child's own environment. The activities and experiments suggested are simple enough for children to conduct themselves, with only a little help from an adult, using objects and materials which will be familiar to them.

Children will gain most from the book if the book is used together with practical activities. Such experiences will help to consolidate knowledge and also suggest new ideas for further exploration and experimentation.

The themes explored in this book include:

Water follows the pull of gravity.
Water fills space.
Water finds its own level.
Water can change its form from liquid to solid.
Water can cause a change in some materials.
Water is essential to life.

Water . . . . .
Tiny amounts
hold together
and form drops.

Big drops run together
and trickle down the window pane.

Trickles flow down a hillside
and join together to form
a rushing stream.

Water naturally flows downhill.
It moves steadily over a gentle slope,
but crashes over a steep one.

Gravity pulls water downward. The force of falling water can be used to work big machines like this water wheel.

Try pouring water onto a water wheel. How can you make the wheel turn faster?

Water fills space.

Pour some into
a glass jar which has
stones at the bottom.
Watch where it goes.

Could you fill
a bottle like this
with water
without filling
the handle
at the same time?

Water cannot flow uphill.
What does it do
when there is something
in its path?

In a fountain
water shoots up in jets.
What makes the water
go upwards?

You can make jets.
Fill a plastic bottle with water.
Point it upright.
How can you make the water
shoot out?

When water is not moving,
its surface is flat and level.

Tilt a container of water
and see what happens
to the level surface.

Water flows.
It is liquid.

But it can change
and become solid.

Where is the water here?

It has frozen into snow and ice.
Look what happens
when snow is warmed.

Water can also seem to disappear
into the air.
When water gets very hot,
it forms tiny droplets in the air.

What is this called?

Steam is hot.
When it touches something cold,
such as this mirror,
the drops of water appear again.

Water can change some dry ingredients.

A little water mixed with flour
makes sticky dough.

What happens when water is mixed with paint powder?

What else mixes with water?

Put paper, sugar,
butter, a brick and salt
into separate glasses of water.
Stir them and watch what happens.

Some liquids mix well with water.

Other liquids do not mix at all.
Look how oil floats
on the surface of this puddle.

There is a skin on the surface of water
which is strong enough
to support small insects.

The skin can stop water from spilling.

People need water
and so do animals and plants.

Water is fun!